Mr. Tony Explores Space

The Young Academics Adventure Series

written by

Anthony Gaskin

Hello, my fellow Young Academics! Today, we are heading for an adventure into outer space! Let's suit up! And while we are preparing to take flight, here are some things to know about space.

"What is the name of our solar system?"

Our solar system is simply call *the solar system* from the word *sol*, meaning sun.

"What is the difference between a galaxy and the universe?"

Think of neighborhoods, then think of the United States. Just like there are many neighborhoods within the United States, there are billions upon billions of galaxies within the universe. I know, kids, a big concept! But so thrilling to think about!

"What is the name of our galaxy?"

Our galaxy is called The Milky Way.

"Is the moon a planet?"

Tricky question! Planets are bodies that hold gases and atmosphere like our Earth, but scientists call the moon an astronomical body—a kind of space debris or waste that orbits the Earth or a star.

"What is a star?"

OUCH! HOT! The sun, which is a star, is one of the most amazing elements in space to me. It is a large body of burning gases. Think of a ball made completely of fire that keeps burning and burning, one which we can never touch.

I am very excited to take you on this journey that we can share with our family and friends!

Lift Off

Okay, are we all suited up? Let's go! First, we will head to the moon and explore some of the characteristics of it, as well as get a great view of Earth. On our way to the moon, we will take a look at the sun from the safety of our ship and will wear protective solar sun glasses to do so. The sun is a star, not a planet. We cannot land on the surface of the sun because, like all stars, it is made of gases—mostly hydrogen and helium—meaning that the surface of the sun is not solid like you would find on Earth or Mars.

The surface of the sun is the hottest element we know of, at about 27,000,000 degrees Fahrenheit. The sun is 864,400 miles (1,391,000 kilometers) across. This is about 109 times the diameter of Earth. The sun weighs about 333,000 times as much as Earth and it takes a whole year for the Earth to rotate around the sun. And, here, my fellow Young Academics, is an interesting fact; the sun is so large that almost 1,300,000 planet Earths can fit inside of it! Imagine that!

Now that we are on the moon, let's take a look at some of its features. What do we notice? Look around; what do you see?

"There are large holes in the ground."

Yes, those are called craters and they were created when meteorites, asteroids, and comets struck its surface at speeds of 10-20 kilometers per second, or 18 miles per second. Craters record the moon's 4.5-billion-year history. In other words, very large rocks—sometimes the size of cars and buses—will crash onto the moon's surface, creating these holes or craters. I love the moon; it is so calming and mysterious, but, sometimes, a full moon is as bright as the sun on Earth.

Let's take a look at Earth from this dramatic vantage point. Notice all the blue? The ocean covers more than 70 percent of the surface of our planet. It's hard to imagine, but about 97 percent of the Earth's water can be found in our oceans, about 2 percent is frozen in glaciers and ice caps. We need to remember that water is very precious to life on Earth, a resource we need to live and grow. What are some of your questions about Earth?

"How big is Earth?"
It is about 24,900 miles in size.

"Does Earth move?"
Great question! Yes, Earth moves—or rotates—around the sun.

Have you ever ridden a rock the size of a bus? Well, our next stop will be the asteroid belt. This region—or area—of space is made up of debris from other meteorites and asteroids colliding into each other, leftover remnants of planets that were formed millions of years ago. As you will see, some of these rocks are as big as small houses, thus allowing us to land on them. Others are as small as toy cars and trains—how exciting is that?!

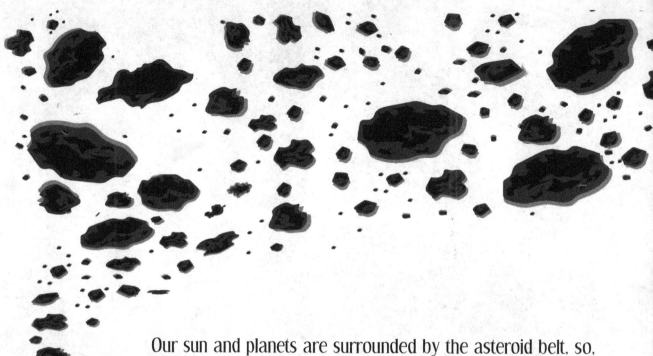

Our sun and planets are surrounded by the asteroid belt, so, as of this moment, we are standing between the outer planets—Jupiter, Saturn, Neptune, and Uranus—and the inner planets—Mercury, Venus, Earth, and Mars. Wow, Young Academics! Isn't this cool?!

"So cool, Mr. Tony!"

It was great to visit the asteroid belt, but now we are headed to Mars, also known as the Red Planet. The reason Mars is so red is because the rock and soil of Mars are rich in iron-oxide.

"What is iron oxide?"
Iron oxide is a film created when oxygen and water in the air react with the iron in metal that has been left out in the rain.

"Mr. Tony, can we live on Mars?"
Not at this time, but scientists are working on a technology called MOXIE (Mars Oxygen In situ resource utilization Experiment). It is an exploration technology experiment that will produce a small amount of pure oxygen from Martian atmospheric carbon dioxide in a process called solid oxide electrolysis. The model will be aboard the Mars 2020 rover mission.

The International Space Station is a large spacecraft in orbit around Earth. It serves as a home base where crews from different nations work together as astronauts and cosmonauts to gather information about space. The Space Station is also a unique science laboratory. Several nations worked together to build and use the Space Station.

What are some of your questions about the space station?

"How long can someone live in the Space Station?"

Awesome question! Let's ask our scientist and fellow astronaut, Ms. Maria.

"We are allowed to stay on board the Alpha Station for six months," says Ms. Maria.

"How big is the Space Station?"

Wow, kids, that is one of the questions I wanted to ask!

"The Space Station is very big. It is approximately 356 feet (109 meters) by 240 feet (73 meters), or slightly larger than a football field," says Ms. Maria.

Since we are all familiar with the size of a football field, that should give you all a good idea of the size of this ship.

Ms. Maria, we are excited to hear about some of the updates you may have for us regarding Mars.

"We have rover vehicles that we send to Mars to collect specimens and take pictures of the Martian landscape. With this information, we can develop better technology to serve our efforts for research and plan our eventual landing on Mars."

What are we doing to find out what makes up the interior of Mars?
"Mr. Tony, I am glad you asked because it just so happens that NASA is preparing to launch a spacecraft to Mars that will land on the surface. This spacecraft, called InSight, for Interior Exploration using Seismic Investigations, Geodesy, and Heat Transport, will launch from aboard a United Launch Alliance (ULA) Atlas V rocket. InSight will study the deep interior of Mars to learn how all rocky planets formed, including Earth and its moon. The lander's instruments include a seismometer to detect marsquakes and a probe that will monitor the flow of heat from the planet's interior.

My fellow Young Academics, can we all say thank you to Ms. Maria for a great visit to the International Space Station?

"Thank you, Ms. Maria!"

Now, off we go!

My fellow Young Academics, that was an exciting visit to the International Space Station! It gave us a little insight into the importance of the work scientists are doing to help us better understand space and our place in it. Now, let's head to our spacecraft to return to Earth!

Mr. Tony and his Young Academics would like to thank you all for your support and encouragement during this amazing adventure into space.

About The Author

My personal story is long and complex, a life full of dramatic ups and downs, triumphs and epic disappointments. I decided to take those, what I call *ingredients of a life*, and use them to create who I am now, a man built on life's lessons. I am an African American male, age 58, and a teacher at the early elementary level, but a teacher to all ages. I graduated in 2017 from SUNY at Empire State College with a Bachelor of Science in Early Childhood Development. I decided to return to school after years of exploring and excavating the meaning of life—or my idea of it anyway. I have always been an academic with bold ideas and ambitions. My book is not just a book; it is a project to help usher in a new era of visuals for young people to help them see themselves in a positive light and engaging narratives. I am no longer settling for children's books, visuals or schools that are not inclusive and nurturing in their dialogue when teaching. My premise is to have characters and story lines that will included a diverse global framework; this will also include children with physical challenges as well—children who have, for far too long, been left out of the collective narrative of learning and mainstream inclusion. In today's book market, you can no longer stop at the book-publishing phase, but now have to plan for a multi-platform approach to a project. I envision this book series to morph into a streaming, animated-learning children's show, not only for children, but also for the whole family. I also plan to develop learning apps based on the original concept of a global, multicultural inclusivity approach to learning and education. In addition to The Young Academics Adventure Series, I have written an essay included in *William Baker Rand Four Decades Essay by Rene Ricard* (published 2018 Osprey Press, pages 122-125, https://www.printedmatter.org). I approached the paintings I wrote about by examining my own life and the historic timeline of my ancestors to express my views on race, struggle and hope..

Anthony Gaskin
Bronx, New York 10457

About The Illustrator

Since receiving his Bachelor of Fine Arts degree from the School of Visual Arts (SVA) in New York City, Nick Meola has been a driving creative force in the licensed apparel industry. Employed by a major childrenswear company for a decade, Nick's uniquely conceptual imagery has continued to win him the acclaim of such industry leaders as Walt Disney, Nickelodeon, Marvel Comics, and Warner Bros.

As a freelance illustrator since the '90s, he has become a nationally recognized character illustrator. His satirically inspired caricatures are featured in a predominate monthly music publication. Nick's network of freelance clients range from advertising agencies, consumer product companies, book authors, an automotive decal company, and music industry labels.

While primarily working in digital media, Nick's artistic styling, combining both his traditional fine arts training and innovative digital art skills, results in a unique style suitable for apparel, editorial, consumer products, and corporate illustration clients.

From classic children's imagery that evokes a nostalgic sentiment to edgy urban designs that are best described as provocative, his visuals are dramatic, effective, and have high-impact results.

Acknowledgments

I want to thank all the family and friends who started this journey with me. There are so many to acknowledge. I want to start with a Thank You to my mom and dad, Ruth Terry Gaskin and Hosea Gaskin, both amazing people who never gave any of their children any word of discouragement, not one! Any idea we had was possible! Thank you, Mom and Dad, for that.

To all the early benefactors and supporters, you all have been instrumental in furthering this project along the path of completion! To the nice young people, Jack and Gemma H. Thank you both for the Tonities pep talk to keep going! And to Maria C. for her friendship and belief in the project.

To all the young children of the world, this is for you to know that, no matter the hurdles in front of you, always think big and reach high.

CPSIA information can be obtained
at www.ICGtesting.com
Printed in the USA
BVHW012139181120
593692BV00001B/1